Enola Marie Lemon

Reflections of Life

A Heart's Story

Enola Marie Lemon

Pearly Gates Publishing, LLC, Houston, TX (USA)

Reflections of Life:
A Heart's Story

Copyright © 2020
Enola Marie Lemon

All Rights Reserved.
No portion of this publication may be reproduced, stored in an electronic system, or transmitted in any form or by any means (electronic, mechanical, photocopy, recording, or otherwise) without written permission from the author or publisher. Brief quotations may be used in literary reviews.

Print ISBN 13: 978-1-948853-02-6
Digital ISBN 13: 978-1-948853-03-3
Library of Congress Control Number: 2020915714

Scripture references are taken from the New International Version (NIV) and King James Version (KJV) of the Holy Bible and used with permission from Zondervan at Biblegateway.com. Public Domain.

For information and bulk ordering, contact:
Pearly Gates Publishing, LLC
Angela Edwards, CEO
P.O. Box 62287
Houston, TX 77205
BestSeller@PearlyGatesPublishing.com

Enola Marie Lemon

DEDICATION

**I dedicate this book to
GOD
and
My Entire Family.**

ACKNOWLEDGMENTS

To Jesus Christ: God has been my guide, my inspiration, and my strength throughout this journey we call "life." Every time I ever picked up a pen or pencil to write every page of this book, He's been the first I go to in prayer, as I asked for Him to lead me with the words I should say and how I should use them. I believe there is no one greater to receive true guidance from than our Heavenly Father.

To my Mother, Marie Lemon: Just thinking about you brings a smile to my face. In the past, our relationship wasn't the best, but with forgiveness and love, all things are possible. I truly thank God for mending the best threads of our mother-daughter relationship. You have been through your own set of challenges in life, but I admire how you haven't allowed those experiences to define you. You are an awesome mother who would do anything for your children. I'm grateful God allowed me to see victory beyond the vision of my past.

To my Stepfather, Samuel Narcisse: You are, without a doubt, my dad. I've never looked at you as a stepfather, although my biological father was greatly in my life. You have shown me who a hardworking father really is. You've never treated me like a stepchild; therefore, I've never felt like one. You have come to my rescue many times from a good butt-whooping (LOL) because Rita didn't play! Any time one of your children—old or young—needed anything, you've been the provider.

To my Children—Trevion Tyrone Lemon, Trevon Blake Lemon, and Nyla Markel Trahan: You are all the joys of my heart and the reason I work so hard at being the best me that I can be. I strive to be a great example for you, just as others were for me. I pray daily that you all come to an understanding of who you truly are and what the meaning of forgiveness is. I also pray daily that God gives each of you a bond with each other that can never be broken because the love is there. If you have love, you can overcome anything. Last but not least, I pray to see the day when God shows my three "caterpillars" what strong and beautiful butterflies you truly are.

To my Brothers and Sisters: God has truly given me some of the best siblings one could ever ask for (I actually prayed for one of them)! LOL! In December 1992, I prayed my mom would give me a little sister, although I had one by my dad who I didn't get to see as often as I would've liked. So, God answered my prayer, and my mom gave birth to a baby girl named **Samantha** in September 1993—two weeks and two days after my 14th birthday. At times, she can be extremely funny and make you laugh until you cry. Even though she's not that cute, little baby anymore, she's still the joy of my heart. Seeing the blessing and the power of prayer, I knew I could always go to God in prayer and have faith in Him to do just what He said he would do.

My other little sister, **Eliza**, is also a blessing sent from God. When God created her, He gave her such a strong ability to express love for her family and the things she loves to do, especially for music.

Reflections of Life: A Heart's Story

My big brother, **Troy**, reminds me so much of our late father. He has a great heart but don't take no mess! LOL! Troy has been great at sports, works hard, and is an amazing father to his girls whom he trained and guided to be their best. I can still remember the smile on my face the first time I heard him sing and thought, "No one could do it better!" (I was young at the time. LOL!)

My brothers, **Peter** (the hard worker and father) and **Jeremy** (the singer, hard worker, and father), are the true definition of "big brothers." They've always shown a great sense of protection for me and have never been afraid to let it be known to everyone. They are their father's sons! LOL!

My brother, **Gary**—although younger than I—has that same protectiveness. I can recall a time in school when he stood up to a boy five to six years older than him. Gary was a lil' shorty then, but that in no way stopped him. The kid was my age, so big sister was the one who beat him up that day. LOL! I can say Gary is my best friend. We've always talked about everything and been a great support to one another throughout life. My sister-in-law, **Amanda**, is like having a relationship with another blood sister. I can talk to her and love that she's not one-sided. She gives me the truth, regardless if it's not what I want to hear. She's helped me through so many challenges and heartbreaks, even while dealing with her own. She's an awesome woman and great encourager. She and Gary are blessed to have one another. I pray God continues to strengthen them with a long life together.

My brother, **Scott**, isn't the youngest, but he is the youngest boy and one of the greatest joys I can recall from when he was a baby. I just loved the way he was so chubby and cute. I would carry him around on my hip all day. I was so skinny at the time, I'm surprised my hip didn't get stuck to one side! LOL! Scott is now taller than I and a very handsome young man. If my boys or I need to know anything about a sports game, team, or the best players—whether it's tennis, football, basketball, soccer, wrestling, or boxing—Scott is our go-to guy for the answer!

I have a great love for all my brothers and sisters, and I know they love me as well. I couldn't imagine a life without any of them. It gives me great joy knowing we can call each other any time and have the support we need without being judged.

To my Auntie Maydell Silas JohnLewis: Wow! I don't believe there are enough words in the dictionary to express how grateful I am for my Aunt Maydell. She is always the first person I call whenever I'm going through something or just to have a laugh and talk about our day. She's a great woman of God and spiritual advisor. She always sees the best in people and knows how to pray for others. One funny fact: She can't pass up a cookie jar without eating one. LOL!

To Overseer Ricky and Pastor Alice Lemon: Overseer Ricky is the greatest man of God I know. He can sing and preach the roof off any building and isn't afraid to share his testimony. He will show you his heart, but you will never see his scars because God has covered every one of them with His blood. People may never see all the hard work his physical and spiritual man endures, but I know he gives it 1,010% without a second thought. It's not because of who he is but rather because of who God is in him and to him. Pastor Alice has a spiritual connection with God that is so strong, she can look inside of a person and draw out just what God gives her for that individual. She's a very confident woman of God and appreciates order. Pastor is never afraid to stand on what she believes in and has no problem chasing any unclean spirit back to the pits of Hell. She and Overseer are a mightily anointed team that has overcome many obstacles and will continue to do so by God's grace. They are my Spiritual Father and Mother in Christ whom I trust with every word God has given them for His people at Radical Praise where, if you don't know what else to do, "Just Give God a Radical Praise!"

To Pastor Keon Henderson: Pastor Keon has been a great leader since I've had the honor of attending The Lighthouse Church of Houston. I relocated to Humble, Texas, in April 2018, but before moving, I remember seeing Mrs. Martha Berry (who is also a member) post a video on Facebook. I recall her being overjoyed about the Word of God that was brought forth that day. Well, I asked Martha, "What church is that?", because when someone is that excited about God, you sometimes just want to experience a little bit of that for yourself—especially coming from Radical Praise where I was so used to praising God, I knew I would feel right at home. I definitely did and have been attending ever since. I love the realness of Pastor Keon and how he's so down-to-earth. It's easy to see he has a big heart for the people but most of all, for Jesus. I remember his sermon titled "20/20 Vision." I'd been wanting to put my book together and get it published, but I was procrastinating. After that sermon, I was more determined than ever and began to get to work. I love the words he used in another sermon that said, "Being a servant of God is my highest honor," and "If it ain't working on me, then I can't give it to you," and also,

"Don't allow your insecurities to speak to your emotions." I believe those three quotes can be life-changing, as they show the character of the man of God I decided to follow because of who he's following.

To my Cousin, Katina Miller: When Katina and I were younger, we would fight like cats and dogs, until the day our grandmother (Ms. Enola) made us wash dishes together. One of us would wash, and the other would rinse. I believe that somehow began to create a bond between us by demonstrating we were on the same team (even though I still think I was grandmother's favorite). LOL! Katina and I did a lot of "dirt" together (I dare not put just what in print form). When I found God, she came along with me and had her own experience as well. I love all my cousins, but everyone knows Enola and Katina were a duo. We've lived together and had the best times, prayed together, and sang together at home and in church because none of our other cousins could (but they tried)! LOL! Oh...That was until our little cousin, Karimah, came along and blew us both out the box. Katina is the Godmother of my twin boys. Even though she's family, she's also my best friend.

To my Best Friends—Chiquita Porter-Ruffin and Elnora Johnlouis: My two best friends aren't acquainted with one another; they just know the lovely me. **Chiquita** and I have been thick as thieves since the day we met in 2006, both working as nurses in Franklin, Louisiana. We're more like sisters and no matter how much or how minimum we talk, our love for each other remains. We can always just pick up where we left off. She's a great friend, mother, daughter, sister, and wife who will put you in your place when it comes to her family. LOL! She's one of the hardest-working women I know, and I'm so very proud of her for getting her Registered Nurse license. Knowing what I know about her, she won't stop there! She's 100% a go-getter and a fighter for who and what she loves.

What can I say about my girl, **Elnora**? "Nookie" and I have known each other since elementary school, growing up in Jeanerette, Louisiana. We must have met when we were six or seven years old but we didn't become friends until we were teenagers. We did other things in life and even moved away for a while but when we reunited, we became closer in our young adult years (hey, we're still young)! LOL! What am I talking about? My friend, of course! I promise you this: Nobody better ever mess with either of our families because Nookie is surely coming to look for you! LOL! Seriously, though: She's just the best and will tell you that she is. She is one who would take my side, regardless whether I'm right or wrong. If I tell her I cussed someone out (because I typically don't cuss), then she'll say, "Well, friend, you must've had a reason!" I thank God that He gave her what she so desired: her little girl. Writing this is making me miss my friends even more. I love y'all!

To my Father, Glen Ferguson: My dad was the funniest yet most serious person I knew. He made me laugh every time I saw him. He could look a man right in the face so serious, then turn to me and smile. He would travel near or far just to see about me. We used to wrestle and have so much fun when I was younger. Even being older, he would sing and dance for me, just to see me smile. He was never a very affectionate person, but everyone knew he loved his children and family.

The first time I ever saw my dad cry was at his mother's funeral (Grandma Eliza). Another time was when my Aunt Dorine fell ill and was in the hospital. Dad was hard on some, but he meant every bit of good and wouldn't stand for foolishness. I'm very grateful to God that my father had a chance to meet and hold all my children before God called him home. In my heart, he will always be the best. R.I.P., Dad.

To my Grandmothers—Enola Washington Silas and Eliza Jones Ferguson: From what I can remember, my grandmothers were very much alike (my little sister was named after Grandma Liza). **Grandma Liza** was a very sweet and quiet woman. My mom told me she was always for someone doing the right thing, whether her own children or relatives. I remember her beautiful smile and how she was always so happy to see me. I surely felt the same.

My **Ms. Enola**—whom I'm named after—was also the sweetest woman, with a smile that could light up the room. She took me to church at a very young age, and I'll never forget experiencing that with her. She was modest and meek, yet firm when she had to be. She had a big family but also a big heart for every one of us. She was the person I looked up to the most and, when I moved back home in 2006, it was always she and I, riding somewhere or going to her doctors' appointments. She and I already loved each other to the fullest, but our bond grew stronger, as I was her favorite. LOL! Tuttima couldn't even take my place! LOL! I can truly say I'm more like my grandmothers than anyone, and God gave me two of the best. R.I.P., My Sweet Ladies.

To my Lil' Cousin, Da'Vonta R. Lemon: I thought I must have been having a bad dream when Carolyn called to tell me of your passing. You were like another son to me and I couldn't help but to think that if I somehow knew about your accident, I could have encouraged you to go to the hospital. However, God's will cannot be questioned by our "what-ifs." You were a great, respectful young man about to start welding school. I know you would have been an amazing welder. You stood for what was right and couldn't stand it when "the little guy" got picked on, even though it sometimes got you into trouble. LOL! You were your mom's best friend, and she'll forever cherish the day you came into her life, as will we all. R.I.P., "D." We miss you more than you'll ever know.

Enola Marie Lemon

PROLOGUE

I've been writing poetry throughout my life for as long as I can remember. At a young age, I realized I could use writing as a way to escape into my own world and express any thoughts or emotions I felt within.

As a young girl, I endured many difficult and inappropriate actions that were inflicted upon me from family members I loved and trusted. On my really bad days, I wanted to disappear. Other times, I had continuous thoughts of committing suicide or hurting those who hurt me. I was screaming on the inside, but nothing could escape my lips.

The day came when I picked up pen and paper and I started penning those things I was afraid to tell my father were happening to his baby girl. It was as if the words seemed to fill up my belly, and I began to write…and write…and write.

Today, I still look back at those words — my words…a child's words. Even though I read and reflect on the hurt, pain, letdowns, and lost trust, I now see I am reading about my strength, forgiveness, love, the will to never give up, being an overcomer, and how profound it was that God placed the words within me at a young age to encourage myself while becoming and encourager.

I always pray before I write. I ask God to give me what He would have for me to write. My heart's desire is to help others because I have realized through it all, He has always been with me. My pain was never meant to destroy me; rather, it was to establish my strength to uplift another. After all, how could I pick you up if I am weak? I write because through God, my footprints are engraved in victory!

Enola Marie Lemon

Reflections of Life: A Heart's Story

TABLE OF CONTENTS

DEDICATION	vi
ACKNOWLEDGMENTS	vii
PROLOGUE	xvi
Introduction	xxi
Faith	1
This, Too, Shall Pass	2
Spiritual Growth	3
A Piece of Me	4
Isn't It Sweet?	6
A Pastor Committed to His Calling	8
God is Calling	10
Somebody in Christ	11
Dead Man > It's Time to Live	13
Earthly Love	15
My Yesterday	16
Love	17
I Don't Love You Enough to Stay	18
Family	20
Thank You	21
Why Is It Scary (Black Mother)?	22
Don't Ever Doubt	24
My Brother's Keeper	26
It Was Always You	28
To My Sister-in-Law on Her Birthday	30
My Heart	32

Little Black Girl	33
Sexual Abuse	34
Dear You	35
Forgiveness	37
I Forgive You	38
God — Love — Forgiveness	40
Spiritual Warfare	41
Wake Up	42
I Pray	44
Endure	46
It Almost Had Me	48
Sleeping in a Storm	50
In My Younger Days	52
Salvation	53
It Is Written	54
This Is War	55
I Choose You	57
You Are My Gift	58
Sorrow	59
Never Goodbye	60
This Day	61
Today Is the Day	62
I'll Look for You	64
Mother-Daughter Duo	66
Signs	67
I'm Here	70

INTRODUCTION

We all hear from God in one way or another. It's up to us to choose to listen. I've tried to understand why some people have chosen not to follow Jesus. Still, I've come to an understanding that the question is an internal understanding for those individuals alone. As for me, I have a thorough understanding of the reason why I love and follow Christ. He's a man who bled and died for my sins and the sins of others. With one drop of His blood, all our sins have been washed away. Then, He rose with all power in His hands! I believe it because death could not bury nor contain the love He has for us. God loves us that much!

On the other side of it all is Satan. He has come to steal, kill, and destroy because he loves watching us suffer. He loves when we give in. He loves seeing us fail. He loves when we choose to follow him and lose our souls in the process. Satan can't stand Christians because God loves us very much—something he once had but lost. Our soul is the one thing that God has given us that is ours forever. It's who we are. However, how we live predetermines where our soul will spend eternity.

There's nothing wrong with changing your life for the better and truly coming to an understanding of our Creator. Great revelations can guide and reveal to you your true destiny. There comes a time when, for us as people, a family, or even as a church, when we must wake up and stop being Satan's puppets. It's time to come together as a true body of Christ to break the strongholds, come out of bondage, and trample on the devil's head for our children and our children's children. Satan is only an illusionist. Therefore, he has no real power—unless you allow his delusions into your mind.

We have all sinned and given into Satan at one time or another, but we can overcome all things through Christ Jesus which strengthens us. Jesus may not be visible in the natural right now, but we can see His works, we can feel Him within, and we can hear Him if we allow Him to speak. No sin is so great that God can't forgive us. No sin is greater than another.

We are God's children, and He loves us unconditionally. On that great day of His return, we will finally see Him face-to-face. Would you want to hear Him say to you, "Depart from me, you workers of iniquity, for I never knew you"? Imagine for just a moment what that would feel like…to be denied by the Father who breathes life into us daily, especially when He has given us so much time to live right. Also imagine not just losing His breath from our bodies, but also from the life of our soul. God has sacrificed His Only Son, yet He doesn't ask us to do the same. All we must do is sacrifice our flesh—that which is not eternal—to save that which is eternal: our soul. God knows we're not perfect, yet we're perfectly forgiven by Him.

God has given us the free will to choose, so why not choose Him?

Reflections of Life: A Heart's Story

FAITH

Enola Marie Lemon

This, Too, Shall Pass

When your heart hurts and it aches,
Only God can mend that break.
No man nor woman, nor friend nor foe
Can water a dead heart enough to grow.

It may take months; it may even take years,
But trust and believe God will dry every tear.
His teardrops carry the strength which makes you whole,
And His love is all you need to keep from going cold.

So, be strong, Enola, 'cause this, too, shall pass.
God will mend your broken heart with protection,
Like a red rose blooming out of green grass.

Psalm 147:3
"He heals the broken-hearted and bandages their wounds."

#AnotherBrokenHeart

SPIRITUAL GROWTH

Enola Marie Lemon

A Piece of Me

Mind filled with thoughts of life.
My brain racing as fast as the cut of a knife.
A heart surrounded with intense emotions.
Tears running down my face as smooth as lotion.

Wondering inside: Lord, when will I ever find that missing piece of me?
For he has taken away his love and now, I am no longer we.
Then, I hear the laughter of people all around,
And for just one moment, my heart and mind are clear of sad sound.

I feel free — free from all the hurt and pain
And life's mistakes that make you feel small.
By cornering you face-to-face
With the illusion of life's dry wall.

(Thinking) I've lost so many pieces of me along the way,
But still, I thank God for the woman I am today.
And then again,
Tapping one foot as my head hangs low,
Feeling and saying, Lord, I'm sorry I hurt You so,
When all You did was bless me and I wasn't worthy of any;
Realizing mistake after mistake! How could I make so many?

So, forgive me, Father, for ever giving up when facing a dark cloud,
'Cause I want to stand strong and always make You proud.
Never putting man or things in Your place alone,
For You are my King sitting on the right-hand throne.

Lord, I need You in my life, You see,
To help me grow into the spiritual woman you've called me to be.
'Cause I know if it weren't for the trials and storms you allowed me to go through,
How would I have ever found the missing piece of me that was truly You?

Jeremiah 29:12-13
"Then shall ye call upon me, and ye shall go and pray unto me, and I will hearken unto you. And ye shall seek me, and find me, when ye shall search for me with all your heart."

#FindingTrueLoveInGodNotMan

Enola Marie Lemon

Isn't It Sweet?

Isn't it sweet to be at peace with life
And experience the joy instead of pain and strife?
To feel the wholeness of your heart,
Which you had from the very start?
To smell the flowers in the air,
And watch their beauty in your care?

Isn't it sweet to find within who you really are
After the healing of a scar?
When you thought being alone was a crying shame,
But out of the ashes, your true self came?
Opening your mind to the greatness you're capable of,
While His peace sits on you, like the grace of a dove?

Isn't it sweet to not fear what tomorrow may bring,
But even in Winter, look forward to Spring?
Or even changing your hair a different color,
Then taking a long walk in the park with your mother?
Maybe you'll make a new friend today
Or climb a mountain to watch the sunset lay.

Isn't it sweet to have your life, health, and strength,
When one day, you didn't know what a blessing this meant?
Having the breath of life in our body;
Thanking the man upstairs, this isn't a hobby.
Knowing you have to give and deserve to be loved,
And all you need comes from above.
Because if someone else takes theirs away,
You already had all you needed, anyway.

So, being alone can be very sweet,
'Cause now you can see clearly, the path of your own feet.

Isn't it sweet?

Jeremiah 15:16
"Your words were found, and I ate them, and your words was to me the joy and rejoicing of my heart; for I am called by your name, O Lord God of hosts."

Enola Marie Lemon

A Pastor Committed to His Calling

On that one special day,
You gave your life to Christ, then answered to His calling.
Realizing the life you lived
Was in the midst of falling.

So, God sent guidance with structure your way,
Then spoke to you and said, "Here, you shall not stay."
Christ molded you into the Godly man He ordained you to be,
While giving you a vision all others needed to see.

The Lord called you back home for leadership
To draw in souls that were lost.
Driving you to Teach, Preach, and Reach
At all cost.

We know the work you do for God
Could never be in vain,
When winning souls for Christ
Is your ultimate aim.

So, we say to you Pastors, on this day:
See God in every new beginning
And continue letting Him lead the way.

1 Kings 8:61
"Let your heart therefore be wholly devoted to the Lord our God, to walk in His statutes and to keep His commandments, as at this day."

Reflections of Life: A Heart's Story

Romans 6:17
"But thanks be to God that though you were slaves of sin, you became obedient from the heart to that form of teaching to which you were committed…"

#ForMyPastors — Overseer Ricky & Pastor Alice Lemon

Enola Marie Lemon

God is Calling

I heard the voice of God last night.
He said, "Listen well, so you may get this right.
I'm calling all women to their rightful roles,
So that they may come together in unity as a whole.
Being linked to all wisdom, understanding, and knowledge I have given thee,
While enduring and submitting to all righteousness in Me.
My women of true virtue are who you are,
And your light shines brighter than angel wings on a star.
While weeping and wailing through the days and nights for lost souls,
Your true desire is for all to become whole.
You're more precious than any diamond, gold, or rubies in My sight,
And when you speak, your wholesome tongue is like a Tree of Life."
You have grown in being obedient and submissive in every way.
Listen, can you hear the voice of God today?
He says, "My women of virtue are neither lukewarm nor cold
Because they've answered my calling and taken their rightful roles."

GOD IS CALLING! ARE YOU READY?

Proverbs 31:10
"Who can find a virtuous woman? For her price is far above rubies."

#WomensConference

Somebody in Christ

"What could this feeling be?" she asked.
I feel something is trying to take over me,
Always appearing to be so shy and quiet to everyone else,
But to her, there's a continuous storm inside herself.
Thoughts and emotions of feeling alone and unloved.
Praying to God in need of His help from above.
So, she kneels down on her knees to pray,
As she didn't do before,
Asking God for His guidance and direction
Through her seasoned door.

As she's praying, she feels herself climbing out of the hole the enemy has dug for her,
And somehow feeling stronger than what she once were.
See, Satan recognized she was a spiritual threat
With a powerful influence on anyone she met.
So, he threw different obstacles in her path to knock her off-track,
But God never sleeps nor slumbers; He had His child's back.

To see what the enemy is trying to do
Comes by a spiritual connection with God.
God never gives up on His children,
Neither does He spare the rod.
He knows how to get us back in line
And out of the snares of the enemy.
I know he can do it for you
'Cause He did it for me.

So, recognize the power God has placed within you,
And don't let Satan bully you all your life,
'Cause just as I am, you're also somebody in Christ.

Enola Marie Lemon

Ephesians 4:22-24

"You took off your former way of life, the old self that is corrupted by deceitful desires; you are being renewed in the spirit of your minds; you put on the new self, the one created according to God's likeness in righteousness and purity of the truth."

#OvercomingDepression

Dead Man > It's Time to Live

Dead Man, wake up!
Your soul is crying out!
Oh, what misery it must be
When you're in pain without a mouth.

Walking this earth, yet dead inside,
All because of your sinful pride.
But you refuse to accept Christ's resurrection, death, and birth,
Even though He lived and died to show you what your soul was worth.

What in this world could be more important to you than living?
Sorry to tell you, but wrong partying ain't giving.
It's not giving strength, grace, peace, love, joy, or saving your soul,
But Jesus gives it all, that you'd be made whole.

Dead Man > It's Time to Live

See, even He — with all power in His hands —
Sacrificed Himself to be a mortal man
So that mankind could see the true meaning of love,
And even His mighty throne couldn't keep Him above.

Yes, He came and died,
But He lived twice for you.
It'll be a shame to be able to live,
Yet die without a clue.

Wow, to not truly know the Man who died for your sins
Is like having a bulletproof vest but trusting in your own skin.

Word of advice: Never rely on the flesh
To cover what needs protection.
Christ set the example
Of His mirror reflection.

For the flesh will one day wither away,
But your soul — whether in Heaven or Hell—is here to stay.
So, allow God to cut every chain of bondage
With His spiritual knife,
And while you yet still walk,
He's able to give you life.

DEAD MAN > IT'S TIME TO LIVE!

2 Corinthians 7:10
"For Godly sorrow worketh repentance to salvation not to be repented of: but the sorrow of the world worketh death."

#Receive Salvation

EARTHLY LOVE

Enola Marie Lemon

My Yesterday

I never knew my yesterday would end so soon.
It's like the day starts over with a never-ending moon.
But to his tomorrow, my yesterday has gone,
And night after night, for him, my heart sings a song.

Lord, when will I see the sunshine of my tomorrow?
It seems I'm stuck on time I know is borrowed.
365 days in a year, over and over,
And I could never find tomorrow's four-leaf clover.

'Cause here I stand patiently, waiting on my yesterday,
Even though my yesterday didn't want to stay.
Oh, how can I stop loving whom I love unconditionally,
Even when trying to convince my heart he doesn't love me?

You see "my tomorrow," therefore, I could never truly love you
Because every beat of my heart is stuck to my yesterday like glue.
To "my yesterday," I know your tomorrow has come,
And I wish you all the best, while dancing in your sun.

Job 17:9
"The righteous keep moving forward, and those with clean hands become stronger and stronger."

#MovingOn

Love

One day, love called my name
With a voice so soft, and slowly it came.
I never expected falling into its arms so hard,
Yet sitting light as a feather on a limb without guard.

I'd bet my life on its every word
And trust its wings against mine if I were a bird.
I loved its stature and curly brown hair,
With its gorgeous eyes and the way it smelled.

Then, it whispered, "I love you," into my ear,
And at that moment, I'm in love was clear.
It made me feel special and showed me all the beautiful things I wanted to see,
But then I realized: I couldn't see me.
Wondering why I could never capture the true picture of its heart,
Even though it framed mine from the very start.

I was in love with love and gave it my all.
Then love knocked me down and didn't catch my fall.
So, I've never allowed another whisper so sweet
To come so close to sweep me off my feet.

I'll wait until the day true love gives me its heart picture in a frame,
And at that moment, I'll do the same.

Proverbs 18:22
"He who finds a wife finds a good thing and obtains favor from the Lord."

Enola Marie Lemon

I Don't Love You Enough to Stay

I was basically told, "I don't love you enough to stay,"
As if we were plastic dolls and our relationship mimicked a life of play—
Which isn't even a life at all 'cause the doll has no knowledge it even exists,
And it could never feel the awakening of true love's kiss.

Is this what you meant when you said I'm living in a fantasy world?
Well, I don't know if you've looked at me lately, but I'm far from a little girl.
I'm a woman—a woman who decided to give you a chance and fell in love;
A woman who thought you were the man who'd finally cherish and protect her in times of a flood.
But instead, you ran in fear at the first sign of a storm.
How foolish you must feel, to know there was no cause for alarm.

On our wedding day at the altar, I signed over my heart to you,
But somewhere along the way, you chose to tear that paper and my heart in two.

Being one takes the strength of two people, never willing to fail,
With the husband being the image of head, not the tail.
You see, you gave up the strength to be one, choosing to be weak and free.
You'd rather walk on the fragments of my heart, than to be the king God called you to be.

So, the queen must bear her throne alone, because her king still wants to be a peasant boy,
Not ready to face reality in the real world, while still flirting with savoy.

One day, it'll be too late to reclaim what you've given up at home
Because a true king will have cherished your throne.

Malachi 2:14-15
"But you say, 'Why does he not?' Because the LORD was witness between you and the wife of your youth, to whom you have been faithless, though she is your companion and your wife by covenant."

#LovelessMarriage

Enola Marie Lemon

FAMILY

Thank You

Thank You, Lord, for being with me every step of the way
And somehow always brightening up each and every sad day.

Thank You for my kids—my three angels here on earth—
Who showed me at birth what true love was really worth.

Thank You for my mom and dad; I wouldn't trade them for the world.
Today, I know they're very proud of their first little girl.

I have to say thank You for the strong siblings you've given me,
And whether young or older, I pray in me it's You they see.

Thank You for my grandma, who showed me right from wrong.
It's because of her I'm so spiritually strong.

Lord, I thank You for giving me the family I have today.
I love each one of them in a very special way.

Most of all, I thank You for Your love and salvation,
And for choosing my family and me to be a part of Your creation.

Philippians 1:3
"I thank my God in all my remembrance of you."

#Jesus

Enola Marie Lemon

Why Is It Scary (Black Mother)?

Why is it scary to give a man-child birth,
Then watch as society ignores his worth?
Or when he sits down to tell you
A bully's been beating him and taking his snacks,
But they try to blame him for being brave and fighting back.
Saying his behavior is aggressive—that's ridicule,
When the other kid had to have a reason to shoot up a school.
Why is it scary when your son leaves home from day to day,
Then every minute of every hour, his safe return you pray?
And even when you've raised him right through all this strife,
If he messes up once, they label him for life.

WHY IS IT SCARY (BLACK MAN)?

Why is it scary to wake up and be you?
Being frozen in fear, just to see the color blue.
Not knowing if today is the day that you meet
And end up another black brother dead on the street
By a trigger-happy pig
That, for some lame ass reason, lost his lid.
Never mind being unarmed; all that matters is you're black—
The only excuse he needs to shoot you in your back.
Now, he has the balls to put his knee on your neck,
As if he won't get convicted was somehow bet.
Wow... As if whippings and hangings weren't enough,
But I'm convinced it's your soul he's really trying to crush.
That's why you have to work twice as hard at being the best,
But even when winning, he wishes you were less.
All because you are who he could never be: a strong black man who's afraid of no one,
So, his only weapon now is to use the gun.
See, you've already excelled in talent and education,
Not to mention you're God's superior creation.

Born a true king, made to sit on a throne;
From bondage to freedom, in strength you've grown.
So, never fear again to wake up and be you,
Because a king is a king, by to himself being true.

Matthew 10:29-31
"Are not two sparrows sold for a penny? And not one of them will fall to the ground apart from your father. But even the hairs of your head are all numbered. Fear not, therefore; you are of more value than many sparrows."

Enola Marie Lemon

Don't Ever Doubt

Don't ever doubt that Jesus is the King from whence you came.
He sent you down from Heaven to bear His Holy name.
To be obedient and learn from God, not just of Him;
Letting His Spirit become your backbone daily in this Christian gym.

Don't ever doubt He's placed an awesome gift within you,
And that gift, no doubt, contains a powerful venue
Where you'll give the devil a nervous breakdown,
Locking him in an asylum way beyond the earthly ground.

Don't ever doubt, to stand firm on what is right,
While recognizing your fist or weapons aren't how you fight.
You fight on bended knees each and every day,
When denying temptations of the flesh as you pray.

Don't ever doubt all your battles are won through our One and Only God,
'Cause on this Christian journey, He's our spiritual mob.
Always strive to walk with God far beyond your natural shoe size,
And with every footstep walked, fragments of the strongman dies.

So, last but not least…

Don't ever doubt God's love for you, my sons,
For it's because of your soul the battle was won.
On the 3rd day, God rose Jesus from the grave,
Knowing all along, He had you to save.
He made it possible for you to have eternal life,
For your soul was His vision, and He brought it with a price.

Reflections of Life: A Heart's Story

Proverbs 3:5-7
"Trust in the Lord with all thine heart; and lean not unto thine own understanding. In all thy ways, acknowledge Him, and He shall direct thy paths. Be not wise in thine own eyes; fear the Lord, and depart from evil."

#ForMySons — Trevion Tyrone and Trevon Blake Lemon

Enola Marie Lemon

My Brother's Keeper

"My Brother's Keeper" used to mean something.
Now, all that seems to matter is the color of a head cufflink.
Or nigga, what side of the tracks do you live on,
When the distance is only the size of a small fishing pond?
No more getting along or squabbling out like men,
'Cause those guns done made you weak to lose your life to sin.
Yea, "My Brother's Keeper" definitely ain't the same.
Can you hear the cry of our ancestors' blood crying out in shame?
Or have you forgotten the dirty road they've had to travel,
Whipped, hanged, beaten, and dragged in gravel?
Lives taken daily as another man's possession,
Then you look your brother in the eye and take his life with the same transgression.
Don't think for one second that a weapon makes you strong or even a man,
'Cause you're just another pawn in the enemy's hand.
Our people were a brotherhood that always had each other's back,
Working from sunup to sundown so none of us had to lack.
And this is the repayment they get for the cost of your freedom?
Never thinking their own people would turn around and cheat 'em.
What a heartless and spineless generation this has become,
Spilling the blood of your brothers means no one has won.
Our people have been burying their sons and daughters to senseless crimes for years.
The Red Sea may have just been stained by the blood of our black mothers' tears.
Yes, you may think you're free 'cause you don't have on chains or are sleeping on floors,
But you're walking yourself to right behind jail cell doors.
Or worse, if you lose your life while living in sin,
'Cause you can't shoot your way through Heaven to get in.
Newsflash: There are no wings gained for living in violence,
And I am "My Brother's Keeper," so I won't keep silent.

Our way of living is like putting the chains back on our ancestor's neck
Without any regard to how they worked and sweat.
Now it's time we take those chains off, and bond our love for one another as strong as they are,
To leave for our children and their children the greatest legacy by far.
"Are You Thy Brother's Keeper" is an imprint we must engrave in our heart
With a "Yes, I am!" after, being the most important part.

Psalm 133:1
"Behold, how good and how pleasant it is for brothers to dwell together in unity!"

Enola Marie Lemon

It Was Always You

Mom, first I'd like to say I love you—
The words you tell me every time we speak,
Which may have just been
The first words you tried to teach.

Growing up and coming to an understanding of who you are
Was one of my greatest lessons here on earth by far.
Through all of your trials, hurt, and pain,
The love for your children has always remained.

And even though you didn't always know how to express it,
The painting of your expressions in my mind sits.
I saw the despair of you wanting so much more for your children,
And you'd never stop trying, even if the number of tries was a zillion.

You never wanted to be a failure, and somehow you think you still are.
Well, I'm here to tell you: There's no failure in a star.
Just look at the amazing children you have raised.
For that alone, we all give you praise.

My Queen, you are the first and the greatest love we'll ever know,
And on behalf of us all, I'm speaking it so.
I can now see the true colors of your beautiful soul;
They are ruby red, white, and gold.

Ruby red is the value of your blood running through my veins.
White is the purest of love from your heart I've gained.
Gold represents your strength for never giving up,
Even when a bruise felt more like a cut.

You are the strength that gets me through each rough patch;
The love that no one else in my heart can match.
The blood through Christ, which gave me life,
So when someone asks, "Who's your hero?" I'll never think twice.

I see you through good or bad because no one is perfect.
You are the reason I know that as a woman, I'm worth it.
Now, take these words like flowers and plant them in your heart,
Knowing the beautiful scent of our love will never grow apart.
As a child, I couldn't see the painting as clear as I do today,
So, to my Mom: You are my greatest hero, I must say.

It Was Always You.

Proverbs 31:25
*"Strength and honour are her clothing;
and she shall rejoice in time to come."*

Enola Marie Lemon

To My Sister-in-Law on Her Birthday

I thank God for the day you came into my brother's life,
And on that one special day, you became his wife.
Now, a part of mine as well,
So, to you, on this day, I have something to tell.
Keep on being who you are.
The blessings you desire aren't very far.
Let the grace you possess and bear
Give you peace and more happiness to share.
Kind and true-hearted is your name.
With your strong presence, you can smother any flame.
God has given you the spirit of order and meekness,
But showing others, "Hey, Never Mistake This For A Weakness!"
Willing to risk it all for the people you love so dearly,
Sometimes, you may find yourself feeling a little weary.
But be encouraged, my sister, 'cause even if no one else does, God sees your effort.
And you, being his child, He will never desert.
So, make a commitment in putting God first in whatever you do.
This is my way of saying, "Happy Birthday! I love you!"

A – AMAZING
M – MINDFUL
A – AVAILABLE
N – NEAT
D – DETERMINED
A – AWESOME

Hebrews 10:24-25
"And let us consider how we encourage one another on toward love and good deeds. Let us not give up meeting together, as some are in the habit of doing, but let us encourage one another—and all the more as you see the Day approaching."

Reflections of Life: A Heart's Story

Romans 15:5
"May the God of patience, who gives endurance and encouragement, give you the same attitude of mind toward each other that Christ Jesus had."

#ForMySisterInLaw — Amanda Key Lemon

Enola Marie Lemon

My Heart

My heart can't deny the way I love you so.
From infant to woman, you've watched me grow.
Whenever I needed you, you've always been there
To help and protect me from the things I couldn't bear.

Every day, I thank God for having a grandma like you by my side.
I see why papa loved you and made you his bride.
Within your heart, you hold a special kind of love;
A love that could only be a gift from God up above.

You're the beginning roots of our family tree;
Surely, my heart can't deny the love I have for thee.
What a beautiful woman you are,
And the strongest I've seen by far.

You possess a smile that gives my heart peace within,
And any brokenness I may feel, that smile will always mend.
For you, my heart will always feel this way:
I Love You, Mawma—A Poem to Say Happy Birthday!

1 Corinthians 13:13
"And now these three remain: Faith, Hope, and Love. But the greatest of these is Love."

Ephesians 4:2
"Be completely humble and gentle; be patient, bearing with one another in love."

#InLovingMemoryOfMyGrandma — Enola Washington Silas
SUNRISE: June 6, 1932 ***SUNSET:*** APRIL 10, 2016

Reflections of Life: A Heart's Story

Little Black Girl

Little black girl, don't be shy.
Hold your head up straight and wipe your eyes dry.
Be not weary of what others may say;
Let God handle those people in his own way.

Little black girl, always be proud of who you are
'Cause in your father's eyes, you're surely a star.
Be thankful for every piece of cloth you wear,
And the lovely way your mother combs your hair.

Little black girl, keep on smiling, even when you want to frown,
To keep yourself uplifted in the midst of feeling down.
Get the best education you can out of life.
Don't ever let them see you quit in strife.
Carry yourself with respect, as a lady should,
'Cause if you don't, then no one else would.

Little black girl, do your best in whatever you do,
For there can only be one you.
So, when those days are said and gone,
You can be at peace when God calls you home.

1 Peter 3:3-4
"Do not let your adorning be external—the braiding of hair and putting on of gold jewelry, or the clothing you wear—but let your adorning be the hidden person of the heart with the imperishable beauty of a gentle and quiet spirit, which in God's sigh is very precious."

Colossians 3:17
"And whatsoever ye do in word or deed, do all in the name of the Lord Jesus, giving thanks to God and the Father by Him."

#ForMyDaughter — Nyla Markel Trahan

Enola Marie Lemon

SEXUAL ABUSE

Dear You

Dear You,
When I fell asleep that night, I thought I was safe,
Only to be awoken by your familiar face.
A face I trusted with everything in me
And through that one act, became my worst enemy.
I was only 12, while you were a grown man
Who invaded my innocence with one touch of your hands.
You were the one who was supposed to protect me from all harm.
Instead, you became the monster by whom I was scorn.

Dear You,
You must know you've forever changed my life
'Cause every thought of that night cuts deep, like sharp blades of a knife.
Do you even understand the damage you've done?
Or was it drink, get drunk, and scar my life for fun?
I'll never comprehend what you were thinking that night.
In shock and disbelief of the whole entire sight.
I wouldn't even care to wish it be a dream
When, in reality, I still couldn't scream.
For son long, all I could feel was hate for you
And if I were big as Goliath, I'd crush you under my shoe.

Dear You,
Although the scars you caused will always remain,
Because of Jesus, my soul is unstained.
I forgive you for the broken girl 25 years ago,
But with my Lord and Savior, that brokenness exists no more.
She's buried by the Holy Spirit and reborn a new queen,
'Cause Heaven is my desire and my soul must remain clean.
So, to the demon that tried to use you to accomplish his goal:
Sorry, not sorry: With God, I remain whole.

Enola Marie Lemon

James 1:12

"Blessed is the one who perseveres under trial because, having stood the test, that person will receive the crown of life that the Lord has promised to those who love Him."

#OvercomingSexualAssault

FORGIVENESS

Enola Marie Lemon

I Forgive You

I forgive you 'cause at the time, maybe you knew not what you do.
From a boy trying to grow into a man, that's true.
But when you left, I already felt like I'd lost it all.
Then, you played on my trust once more and got my guard to fall.
Yea, I Forgive You.

You, for taking that which we created
And trying to cut me out of their lives related to another lady.
I felt empty inside and became lost to myself,
While smiling on the outside but inside, feeling as small as an elf.
Remembering all the nights I laid and cried,
Thinking to myself I'd just lay in my pain and die.
Even calling your mom for comfort when, in reality, it was all a plot.
And she, too, herself, had her very own spot.
Yea, I Forgive You.

But wow, to thinking back: How could I have been so blind?
Maybe blind to the false hope that someday, you'd again be mine.
Enough of that: I know now you didn't love me as a husband should.
But one question, though: What feeling makes a man strip a woman of her motherhood?
I was a good Christian wife and mother who worked hard to feed her family while paying the bills,
But you know one thing I've realized? Satan kills.
Not giving him any credit at all,
'Cause without our willingness, he couldn't allow us to fall.
Yea, I Forgive You.

Lord knows how I'd pray things were different,
But God gives us free will, even in our indifference.
Notice everything we'd hope to accomplish as friends, parents, or husband and wife.
We've now allowed Satan to snatch from our life.
Rewind to the beginning. Do you even remember what the Prophet said?

So now, let's be who we are in Christ, and claim every work of the enemy dead.
Yea, I Forgive You.
Please Forgive Me, Too.

P.S. *It's All For Christ.*

Ephesians 4:32
"And be ye kind one to another, tenderhearted, forgiving one another, even as God for Christ's sake hath forgiven you."

#Forgiveness

Enola Marie Lemon

God — Love — Forgiveness

Love is like the day sun that shines so bright when it's hot
But seems pitch dark in a storm when it's not.
Following the wrong signs will get you lost that way.
Instead of going straight, you knowingly make a U-turn and say,
"Wow, how did we get here? Maybe we both fell asleep somehow
Or got lost in the midst of thick fog-like clouds."
When your actions continually break someone's heart,
This is how repeated wrong turns start.
No need to cut your eyes or point the finger to blame.
It's either one or both of you taking this marriage for a game.
But full circle you must come to be
By letting God give you strength as strong as roots of a tree.
Pain can take you down a very dark road if you allow it to,
But broken love can still be put back together with two.
Forgiveness has to come before you can trust once more,
And putting Jesus first is the key to that door.
You see, when God is not the author of everything in your life,
It gives room to Satan to cause unfaithfulness and strife.
Not saying it's always going to be all peaches and cream,
But your relationship wouldn't be the one you once dreamed.
Listen, neither of you started a life together to be defeated by the enemy;
All things are possible, and Jesus is the remedy.
You held hands and made vows to forever share your love,
But the true vow you made is to our God up above.
So, if you are obedient to this one thing,
He'll give you the strength you need to honor the ring.

Colossians 3:13
"Bear with each other and forgive one another if any of you has a grievance against someone. Forgive as the Lord forgave you."

#GodLoveForgiveness
#Marriage

SPIRITUAL WARFARE

Enola Marie Lemon

Wake Up

Wake up! The enemy's #1 goal is to keep you blind
In knowing who you truly are,
While planting dreams of doubts and disbeliefs
That in life, you're doomed to go far.
See, he laughs at your trials and tribulations
And loves seeing you down,
But it's me who give you victory
To rise from the ground.
Satan has covered your flesh
With his demonic gnats,
And they're eating away at your soul
As a daily snack.

Wake up! They have your ankles wrapped in chains,
With every finger zip-tied with strings.
You're like his little puppet;
He doesn't plan to let go.
Wait. But puppets are fake
And have no say-so.
Now listen, even when covered in mud, you're not dead.
So let go of the trash by the enemy you've been fed.
It's time to stop sleeping in darkness
And find the light I've given thee.
Your soul is calling out because
You've put your flesh as god over me.

Wake up! Pray and use your God-given strength to stay conscious, my child.
Then walk no more with the negative crowds.
For, unlike puppets, you do have a soul,
And your eternal life with me is my ultimate goal.

Wake up! Rise and open thy eyes!

My hands have always been here
To keep you from falling.
I've never left, nor will I ever leave you.
Now, grab hold of my Spirit and step into your true calling.

Zechariah 3:3-4
"Now Joshua was dressed with filthy clothes as he stood before the Angel. So the Angel of the Lord spoke to those standing before him, 'Take off his filthy clothes!' Then, he said to him, 'See, I have removed your guilt from you, and I will clothe you with splendid robes."

#SaveYourSoul

Enola Marie Lemon

I Pray

I pray that you're always prepared—in and out of season—
Because Satan is on your tracks, and I know the reason.
See, you're an awesome vessel for God to use,
And he knows with God's power, his heels you can bruise.
So, he throws out to you his best fishing pole,
Trying to feed you bait that continually stains your soul.
Waiting for the day you're finally trapped on his hook
'Cause he knows feeding your flesh was all it took.
You must think he's your friend because he gives you all the world's lustful desires,
But he's filled with hate for you, waiting patiently for you to hang yourself with his eternal barbwire.
He knows that you're the heir to God's heavenly throne,
So like a homeless dog, he throws you dry bones.
But don't be as a dog and walk mindlessly through oncoming traffic just to get fed,
'Cause every dog that did, one day ended up dead.
See, it's the trick of the enemy to befriend you like he's your main ace or your roun
By giving you what seems to taste good, when his #1 goal is to take your crown.
But I pray. I pray that you always stay on your journey with God,
While recognizing every tactic of Satan in his sleek façade.
Look at yourself in the mirror. You're stronger than what your natural eyes can see.
Now, stop following an imposter and allow God to lead, that your mind and soul may be free.
'Cause Jesus is the only One who can break the chains of bondage in this life.
Without Him, it leaves you subject to the devil's poisoned knife.
With it, he'll cut you time after time with sin until you've lost your soul,
Then leave you in Hell's fire to rot, when you've allowed him to accomplish this goal.

So, don't play victim while allowing the devil to do the crime
Because in this scenario, with your life, you do the time.
But I pray.

1 Peter 5:6-9
"Humble yourselves, therefore, under the mighty hand of God, so that He may exalt you at the proper time, casting all your care on Him, because He cares about you. Be serious! Be Alert! Your adversary the devil is prowling around like a roaring lion, looking for anyone he can devour. Resist him and be firm in the faith."

#PrayerIsAWeapon

Enola Marie Lemon

Endure

When you're in the will of God,
Obstacles shall come your way.
But God says, "Endure, My child,
And try your hardest not to stray.
In this life, nothing is easy;
You may fall sometimes.
But you'll never have to crawl
When I carry a child of Mine."
In the midst of hills and mountains all around,
And it seems your ears have lost their sound…
But Endure.

In the light of day,
Darkness appears to fill the air.
And you ask the question,
"Lord, why so much despair?"
He says, "Endure."

Rough times, trying times, sad times, and times you feel but a lonely man…
But Endure.
It's all in the Master's plan

You see, the fight is fixed,
So your battle is already won
'Cause the enemy's weapon
Is merely a blank gun.
He may bruise you.
He may even knock you down.
But a child of God
Never stays on the ground.

So, Endure 'til the end and I'll save a seat for you on God's heavenly bus
Because remember, God first Endured for us.

2 Timothy 2:10
"Therefore, I endure all things for the elect's sake, that they also may obtain the salvation which is in Christ Jesus with eternal glory."

#YouShallReapIfYouFaintNot

Enola Marie Lemon

It Almost Had Me

Living life as a sinner,
"It" made me feel free.
Free to experience and do the things
I wanted to willingly.
"It" influenced my thoughts
And my every move,
While keeping me blind sighted
To another I could choose.
"Its" ideal goal was to watch me suffer
And lose my soul,
But my Lord and Savior
Had another goal.

"It" almost had me,
Until I looked in the mirror
And didn't recognize who I saw.
At that moment, I knew I was lost.
"It" trapped me in a world of camouflage and delusion,
Putting in my mind strife and confusion.
I felt my spirit man quickly withering away,
But I knew I still had the ultimate weapon, and that was to pray.
To pray effectively to the God I once knew;
Lord, I'm ready to change my life and put all my trust in You.
I'll put this flesh in handcuffs and throw away the key
'Cause every day I walk with Thee is a bridge set in stone to my destiny.

Now, the obstacles may not be easy at all,
But God, I know now you'll never let me fall.
God says, "I've been waiting for this day
'Cause I know you're not perfect.
But I love you unconditionally
And your soul is worth it.

I know it's been hard
And you've even had doubts.
Yes, "It" almost had you, but today,
Almost doesn't count.

1 John 1:9
"If we confess our sins, He is faithful and righteous to forgive us our sins, and cleanse us from all unrighteousness."

#GodDelightsInChangingLives
#IncludingYourOwn

Enola Marie Lemon

Sleeping in a Storm

Isn't it ironic that when it's raining outside,
All we want to do is sleep?
All cuddled in our beds and unaware
Of what crawling things creep.
The blankets feel so clean, warm, and cozy.
Secure in our homes from anyone noisy.

It's sad to know some have the exact same illusion
In the storms of life,
Not realizing that letting some people in
Comes with a price.

But all you saw was the beauty and charm
Of their outward physique,
Not the demon inside
That was rendering you weak.

See, charm is a great weapon the devil uses
To travel from your ears to your brain,
Leaving his spat behind like flies
For his demons to come back and drain.

And you're still sleeping,
Blinded to the lies and dark web he's creating.
Even though your eyes are wide open
But his hold feels sedating.

Now, you're trapped in a storm,
All for some fleshly pleasure,
Without a thought to think
Of what the consequences might measure.

Reflections of Life: A Heart's Story

Sleeping in a storm
Won't just cost you your smile;
You could lose your life, a spouse,
Or your innocent child.
A child you made a choice to leave here and there,
Whose innocence was taken by the one you left to care.
Or trying to play house with another mouse,
When you thought you had the getaway map
And the cheese turned out to be a sleaze,
Catching you in the trap.

Compromising with the devil isn't how he rolls.
You give him an inch, and he'll snatch your soul.
'Cause no matter how warm a blanket may be,
The stains on the mattress still lies,
Just like the stains on your soul
Until you open your eyes.

There's a storm in your life
That's burying you as you still breathe.
This means it's not too late
To arise from the dirt and take heed.

Now, grab a hold of the Peacemaker's hand
And never let go,
Because remember: If you turn back,
Satan's bringing back seven times more.

Luke 8:23 -25

"As they sailed, he fell asleep. A squall came down on the lake, so that the boat was being swamped, and they were in great danger. For whoever wants to save their life will lose it, but whoever loses their life for me will save it. What good is it for someone to gain the whole world, and yet lose or forfeit their very self?"

#HavingFaithInTheStorm

Enola Marie Lemon

In My Younger Days

In my younger days, I had a rough life.
I did bad and crazy things, but never thought twice.
Only because I needed love and attention,
But to my parent, I dare not mention.
Attention that wasn't given to me at home,
And when it was, it was always wrong.
I let the words and actions of others change who I was,
So I accepted fake love and stayed high off bud.
Knowing in my heart that I was a good child
And I could light up a whole room with just one smile.
The words my grandma would always say.
So, why did I get treated this way?
Slapped and punched for the little less things;
Some days I'd wished I had magical wings.
I'd fly away to a happier place—
A place without depression or thoughts of suicide,
Or such anger that was built up
So deep inside.
But I know now that God's grace was upon my life.
Because of Him, I now think twice
About all the things I do and say,
Like the words that come out of my mouth each day.
God is our doctor and there's no wound He can't suture,
So, like me, don't let your past predict your future.
Jesus is the only Salvation for our dying souls,
For us as sinners, on the third day he rose.
Choose now to walk with Christ in every way
And receive Him into your heart today.

Jeremiah 29:11
"'For I know the plans I have for you,' declares the Lord, 'plans of peace and not of evil, to give you a future and a hope.'"

#OvercomingPhysicalAbuse

SALVATION

Enola Marie Lemon

It Is Written

Once upon a time, God in Heaven arranged a marriage for His Son,
And sent out invitations, but no one wanted to come.
So, He placed His Spirit inside of flesh to be born,
To be an example for the sinful and scorn.
He led many of us and taught us all He knew,
But alongside the righteous, there were unbelievers, too.
Denying and questioning everything He'd do or say;
Even one of His own betrayed Him as He pray.

We spit on Him and hit Him with rocks of coal,
Not realizing this was the man who would die for our souls.
He was born as an anchor for our salvation from this worldly sin
Because we couldn't do it for ourselves, and neither could our friends.
God prepared the way so that those who are ready could get to the wedding at the appointed time,
And at the altar, King Jesus we'd find.
God never underestimated the pain Jesus would go through,
But before we were conceived in our mother's womb, God said, "I knew you."

Jesus was sent that we might bee saved, delivered, and set free,
With a sure gateway to Heaven for all who believed to see.
Assuring in Him, His home is our eternal life,
It is written, so today and every day, I choose CHRIST.

1 John 5:12-13
"The one who has the Son has life. The one who doesn't have the Son of God does not have life. I have written these things to you who believe in the name of the Son of God, so that you may know that you have eternal life."

#GodOnEarth

This Is War

This is war, and the requirement is a broken-now-unbroken leader
Who will cover us like needle spikes of a cedar.
These two made one are the best for the job.
Together, they've won many battles against the devil and his so-called mob.
Making sacrifice after sacrifice, while lifting God's people in prayer,
God sent them back home because we needed their care.
You see, being unbroken in spirit is to deny every brokenness of the flesh,
And these two made one are crowned by the best.
They were chosen by God to equip a chosen people.
When He called, they answered "Yes" to, "Are you thy brother's keeper?"
This Is War.

So, today we declare war on the enemy's head
For every lost soul and loved one's blood he's shed;
For a better life here on earth
And every time he's tried to belittle our worth.
But he's the dumbest one to ever exist,
To have Heaven as his home and then be dismissed
Because he chose not to obey God, wanting to be his own boss,
But the fight is a fixed fight, and he's already lost.
Although with God on our side, he's surely defeated;
It doesn't stop his true nature of being conceited.
Radical Praise, our leaders in this war were sent here to be our guides,
While being great examples so that we may get things right while still on this side.
Now, don't sit back, let Satan claim your souls, and drag you to Hell.
Your souls have been bought with a life, and it's not for sale.
And even though in battle, you may get cut or fall down,
As long as you get up, your reward is your crown.
This Is War.

So, to Pastor and Overseer: Keep up the great work God has begun within you
Because you're armed and dangerous, and the devil has a clue.
Your spiritual man is as lethal as a loaded gun,
And Satan knows you don't take this walk with God for fun.
So he tries to hinder you from afar,
But whenever he tries, he's branded with a scar.
It's God's way of telling him, "Touch not my anointed and do my prophet no harm,
Because against these two made one, you are unarmed."
THIS IS WAR!

Luke 10:19
"Look, I have given you the authority to trample on snakes and scorpions and over all the power of the enemy; nothing will ever harm you."

#FightWithFaith

I Choose You

The day I spoke you into your mother's womb, it was so.
My destiny and plans I'd have for you to go.
I choose you—not for what you could do for me, but I for you.
Let your spiritual ears and eyes hear my voice and see the floor plan I've drawn up just for you to do.
The tools you need, I've already placed within.
Now stay prayed up and deny the fleshly sin.
Today, tell Satan and his demon dogs goodbye,
And leave them to rout in the pits where they lie.

I choose you because you're stronger than you know,
And once you realize this, you'll finally see your true growth.
Don't continue settling for the familiar things around
When you're kings and queens, and I've called you to wear a crown.
The plans I have for thee are far greater than your natural eyes can see.
I choose you, as it was designed, to be a part of me.
Trust and believe My words won't return void as an empty page.
Now, stop hiding behind the curtains, when I've called you to be on stage.
For you're only human, and I know temptations will come.
That's why through Me, your victory is already won.
Because with Me, you have power to overcome every stronghold,
But stay hot, My children, not lukewarm or cold.
So, I need you to choose me this day
'Cause flaws and all, I choose you anyway.

1 Peter 2:9
"But you are a chosen race, a royal priesthood, a holy nation, a people for God's own possession, so that you may proclaim the excellencies of Him who has called you out of darkness into His marvelous light."

#NotJustCalledButChosen

Enola Marie Lemon

You Are My Gift

Yes, today is Christmas, when gifts are exchanged from person to person,
When giving out of love, even when uncertain.
Will I receive a gift just for who I am in return,
Or will my sacrifice be tossed in the fiery furnace to burn?
You are my gift, but let me remind you: I was yours first.
It was proven many years ago on this, the day of My birth.
For even though you walked, you were yet still dead—
Until you receive the gift of My life to be spiritually fed.
You see, let's get straight to the point:
My Spirit came here to set free and anoint.
It doesn't matter the place where I was born into this world;
My Father's mission for your souls was never blurred.
Although physically, you may not have what you think you need,
Be grateful for your soul, which I've given My life to be freed.
So, don't purposely put on chains and walk through Hell's double doors,
When you have a Father who saves and restores.
Please listen, My children, as I speak to your hearts:
You are My gift, from whom I never want to depart.
Now, don't let the snares of this world cause you an eternal loss,
When My gift to all was in My birth, death, and resurrection to you without cost.
Surely, My desire is your love and soul to be whole when I come.
Then, I can say, "My child, they good and faithful servant, well done."
So, give Me you as you receive Me 'cause to die for your sins, I never thought twice,
For you are My gift, and I am your Tree of Life.

John 3:16
"For God so loved the world, He gave His Only Son, so that whosoever believe in Him will not perish but have eternal life."

#OurGiftFromGod

SORROW

Enola Marie Lemon

Never Goodbye

I never imagined this is how we'd say goodbye.
You're like far away angels below Heaven's sky.
And while I may not be able to walk with you today,
The memory of our love will always stay.
So, even though I've gained my wings,
I'll be with you in spirit when you exchange rings.
Hugging you around your necks, as I happily remember you hugging mine,
Telling me "I love you, Ya," time after time.
NEVER GOODBYE.

For you are the greatest family God created just for me,
And that showed me just how special I must be.
To have a mom so tough, yet her heart's as soft as cotton:
Mom, God says, "You are not forgotten."
And to have a father who's an awesome leader and provider:
Dad, God says, "You are a survivor."
Then, to have sisters and brothers who are my greatest joy,
They're like having the best real-life toys.
God says to you, "Always follow Me and you'll never go wrong."
We'll all meet again one day to sing our favorite songs.
Never saying goodbye because I'm in your hearts to stay,
So I'll rest in our Savior's arms until you find your way.
NEVER GOODBYE.

Proverbs 17:6
"Children's children are a crown to the aged, and parents are the pride of their children."

RIP Lamara Rashad "Tuk" Lemon
SUNRISE: 8/1/2006   ***SUNSET:*** 5/26/2020

Reflections of Life: A Heart's Story

This Day

My friend, today I know your heart is torn
Because the loss of your mother you mourn.
And there are no words or actions I can say or do,
No matter how much I'd wish to take away that pain for you.
But just know she's smiling down from Heaven with a big kiss to your face.
She's gained her wings and finished her long race.
If she could be with her babies forever, she would;
The bond you all shared was well understood.
But the strong woman she was will always remain
'Cause her strength is in all of you, just the same.
So, let the loving memories of her life shower you down with joy as she's laid to rest on this day,
Knowing she would want it filled with love…exactly this way.

Ruth 2:12
"May the Lord, the God of Israel, under whose wings you have come to take refuge, reward you fully for what you have done."

In Loving Memory of Mrs. Jeanetta Sereal Johnlouis

SUNRISE: 8/4/1946   *SUNSET:* 4/2/2017
#ForMyFriendElnoraJohnlewis

Enola Marie Lemon

Today Is the Day

Today is the day.
I need all my family and friends to listen and hear me well:
It's me—Da'Vonta—and I have a story to tell.
For those of you who knew me, you know I had my own mind.
And when it was made up, you couldn't change it nare time.
I was raised to be strong and I always looked out for others.
That's why my friends aren't just my friends; we're more like brothers.
Today is the day I've learned that Jesus is the key,
And He's shown me all I've needed to see.
So, if I could speak to you all I the natural, I'd say:
Today is the day. It's time we get things right.
My physical eyes may be closed now, but God has given me spiritual sight.
To now see what the enemy is trying to brew,
By creating slangs like "Turn Up," as if it's something fun to do.
God's love for us is far greater than we could ever comprehend,
And every broken spirit He Himself wants to mend.
Mom and Dad, I've seen every tear that's fallen from your face,
But God has given you all the strength you need to endure this emotional race.
And when you feel as if the pain is too hard to bear,
Just let Jesus carry you; He'll always be there.
Right now, my lil' brother's too young to fully understand, so he just goes with the flow,
But hey, he's not too young to be turned onto a God he needs to know.
I'm truly sorry I had to leave this way,
But when my King called my name, I had to obey.
He said, "Da'Vonta Ramon Lemon, today is the day.
The war has begun, and you never leave a fallen man behind,
Especially when that fallen man is spiritually blind."
You see, you only live once (YOLO), so don't let it be in vain.
Today is the day to walk with God while you stand.
Now, on your feet, my soldiers! We were born to be victorious in life.
Never weak but made strong, by the One and Only Christ.

Reflections of Life: A Heart's Story

Romans 10:9
"If you confess with your mouth, 'Jesus is Lord,' and believe in your heart that God raised Him from the dead, you will be saved."

In memory of my Lil' Cousin, Da'Vonta R. Lemon
SUNRISE: 6/11/95   ***SUNSET:*** 10/27/15

Enola Marie Lemon

I'll Look for You

I can recall having a dream that night,
Waking up in sweat and overcame by fright.
You were sitting near a big house on the opposite side of the road,
Waving at me to come, but my feet felt like loads.
Loads of bricks that I could never let go of to get to the other side,
Then, as the dust clears, I see you fadingly wave goodbye.
I'll look for you.

Heart of my heart and blood of my veins,
Taken away so swiftly on the Death Angel's wings.
I never had a chance to wave back goodbye,
But I'll look for you when my clear day turns into black skies.
Strength to my weakness and courage to my fear,
How can I walk in braveness without you here?
You were the joy in my laughter, the rock I could always lean on,
And the true hummingbird that was always eager to sing me a song.
You are my hero without the cape.
Missing you is never a thought I can escape.
And even though older, you somehow looked up to me;
By seeking in me, the Christ you see.
Now, rather smooth with a stare or rough around the edges and loud,
Having you as a father has always made me proud.
I'll look for you.

When my soul has escaped into a faraway place
And you and I are again face to face,
We'll hold hands and sing our favorite song
And encourage all the angels to sing along.
As we dance in the clouds without a care,
Sharing stories of both here and there,
Oh, what a joy this will be!
So, while you're standing at Heaven's Gate, please look for me.
I'll look for you.

Reflections of Life: A Heart's Story

Philippians 2:20
"I have no one else like him, who will show genuine concern for your welfare."

For my Dad, Glen J. Ferguson

SUNRISE: 8/28/1951   *SUNSET:* 8/1/2003

Enola Marie Lemon

MOTHER-DAUGHTER DUO

Signs

Where are you, Heaven, when the sky is blank blue?
Where are the stars you have cried for me to tell me it will be alright?
Through all the pain, there is still beauty left in this life.
Where are the clouds you've laid out for me
To show me that something so soft and vulnerable can all be
So big and mighty?
Where are you, Heaven, when there is no wind to shuffle through the trees?
Where are you to show me that the wind may knock down my leaves, but the trunk of my soul will stand its ground?
Where are you, Heaven? Are you closer than I think or as far as you seem, because right now, you only sound real in my dreams?
A life with no stress, a life without hard times just doesn't sound possible to me.
Where are you, Heaven? Where are you when the cracks under my feet seem wider and wider?
Every day, one foot seems to fall through this cracked earth, bringing me closer and closer to a life of hell.
Where are you, Heaven, when many have told me you were real, but all your beauty to this ugly world cannot be seen?
I want to know you're there and not only in my dreams.
Where are you, Heaven, when there are rainy days but no rainbow to tell me my storm has truly passed?
Where are you? Where are you when my heart that was never prepared to be broken time after time begins to crack like a Haitian sidewalk?
God, where are You when things are going so good but an accidental cut can remind me I can still be broken and there is still pain?
Where are You, God? Where are You when these broken emotions and broken memories consume me faster than faith ever will?
Where are You when the ringing of a bell reminds me of off-tune church bells and body bags, grief, and misery?
God, where are You when I am running in this maze I call my mind, Trying to find my way back to my soul? Where are You?
Where are you, Heaven? Show yourself! Where are you?

Please give me a sign because this life is hard and the most I can do for myself right now is just accept these scars.
Where are you, Heaven, when the night is only there to tell me that those bright, good days will not last forever?
Where are you when the blank sky is just there to tell me even my pain is something it, too, cannot endeavor?
God, where are You? Where are You, hu? Where?
Let me fade into the sky. Let the sun cry to me and tear me piece by piece to renew me.
Let me find myself again. I am lost within me.
Where are you, Heaven, when my spirit finds its way back to me?
But the teardrop is only there to tell me it can't stay for long;
That this body is a shell that is supposed to keep it safe,
But it's also trying to get my soul replaced.
Breathe life into me, Heaven. Give me the signs to show me that my soul is still mine.
Where are you, Heaven, when I want to give up?
Where are you when the allusion I wake up from that we call slumber, just reminds me that I'm still stuck?
How do I make it through this life without you?
My body plays hide-and-seek with my mind and soul, I'm still trying to find myself.
How could I ever do this without you? Don't hide from me, too!
Don't let go like I feel I already have sometimes.
Where are you? Please give me a sign. Please!
Where are you when the thunder outside reminds me another is gone on?
Where are you when a simple touch reminds me of that bed and a touch on the leg to tell him to fight, only for him to tell me he no longer could?
These memories, these daydreaming nightmares, won't go away.
Touch me, Heaven, to remind me of not death, but happiness.
Where are you when all the good memories turn into fantasies?
Help me to remember a life with not only just grief.
Give me a sign you're still there. Just one, Lord. I need Your guidance.
I can no longer do this on my own, in this world with thousands of people, in this building with hundreds but still feel alone.
Are you still there? Are you even real anymore, Heaven?

Because what do I do when even being around people makes me feel like each one of them are sucking the life out of me?

When each breath stops before it could even reach the surface of my tongue?

Where are you, Heaven, when the pounding of a headache reminds me of a warning drum of his heart?

I know he heard before he took his last breath.

Oh, Heaven, come back to me, please.

Did you ever really leave? Or am I just not worthy to see you anymore?

Please, just open your door. Hear me, God. I'm letting you in.

I was lost and I ran away because nothing seems to go right anymore. Help me find myself. Help me find my way back to You.

Help me to remember all Your signs.

I no longer want to be blind. The clouds, the stars, the wind, and the trees… Show me Your signs.

Are you there, Heaven? Were you ever?

Jeremiah 29:13
"You will seek Me and find Me,
when you seek Me with all your heart."

Written By: **Nyla Markel Trahan**
(Daughter)

Enola Marie Lemon

I'm Here

I am the peace that calms the blue sky,
Leaving it blank for you to create what your heart sees inside.
Just look up, my child, and see the stars have always been there,
Even in the darkest night, when your natural eyes cannot see where
My teardrops have fallen
Until you've reached the sea by them created to carry you from crawling.
I'm Here.

Now, you have to understand why you were created.
See, pain and beauty are intentionally related.
Pain really gives you strength and knowledge to see the beauty in this life,
Knowing that with God, if you had victory once, you can have it more than twice.
Can You See?
The clouds are aligned just where I designed them to be,
But your soul is more of a priority to me.
I'm Here. I'm Everywhere.
And just because you don't see the leaves of the tree shuffle, does not mean the wind isn't there.
The wind can blow the strongest of tree to the ground if I allow it to,
But sometimes, I allow the strongest of wind to be still, just for you.
So, yes, my child: I'm closer than I appear,
And the more your soul seems to drift away, I'll be even nearer.
Whether you're dreaming or awake, I'm real;
I come to give, but not one ever questions who actually comes to steal.
I'm Here.

Life was never made to be hard or stressful, but sin brought about change,
And with change, a placed called Hell was arranged.
Sin is the ugly face, for why my beauty cannot be seen,
But if you look with the eyes of your heart, you'll see the true unseen.
And no matter how wide the cracks under your feet may get,

Reflections of Life: A Heart's Story

I'll carry you.
I'll carry you until your blank sky turns colorful blue
And you see the promising rainbow of your tomorrow,
Letting you know the passing of our storm's sorrow.
Sorrow is gone, but My child, I cannot promise you a life free of broken hearts;
I can only promise to be there from the end to the very start.
I'm Here.

In good times or bad, you'll always be a part of Me.
I encourage you to speak to Me openly.
There's no brokenness that I cannot heal.
With My blood and resurrection, this was already sealed.
You must have faith and believe in Me,
Then nothing and no one can have victory over thee.
I'm Here.

Regardless of what church bells may ring,
I've given you the gift of music to sing.
And no worries can overtake the gift you have inside
When your beautiful voice can change hearts worldwide.
Remember, I am the Creator of your mind.
Therefore, it is not void of any unfamiliar twine.
You shall not be afraid of your scars any longer
Because what can't kill you, only makes you stronger.
Listen: I'll always be here.
And you know why?
Because the love I have for you wouldn't allow me to stay in Heaven's sky.
And even through pain and suffering, I loved My fleshly life
Because I was able to purchase your spiritual life with that price.
I'm Here.

I will let you soar above the sky,
Allowing the sun to kiss your face without a burn to make you cry.
I'll watch you grow gracefully, as all beautiful flowers should,
And watch you overcome everything I knew you could.
You'll never have to go through this life alone
Because I am the roots to your cornerstone.

Enola Marie Lemon

And the thunder you hear is the soft roaring of My voice,
For all loved ones before passing has already made a choice.
But be assured, I was there keeping you strong,
And your encouragement to fight was never wrong.
He understood the gentle touch of your hand,
But saw his blue sky departing like sand.
Therefore, no longer by pain rattled
Because he recruited Me to fight his battle.
I'm Here.

Unfortunately, natural death must be faced to get to the other side,
But sadly, spiritual life is often lost because of sinful pride.
Your soul is the greatest gift I have to give,
And the only requirement is to protect it by the life you live.
See, grief is only supposed to be but for a moment;
Memories are a lifetime.
So don't allow a moment to take away life's sunshine.
You are gorgeously, gracefully, and amazingly made.
Not one of those words describes afraid.
I'm Here.

It's time to see Me and wipe away the blur.
People are only distractions to stop you from seeing her.
In a mirror, clear as day,
Trap every bad thought behind My garment to stay.
And hold your head up; I made you to be proud.
Your presence alone creates its own crowd.
Worthy is a person notable and important with great qualities,
And that you are—on every level.
That's why I've gone through death and high waters to keep you from the devil.
I'm Here.

Lost? No, you were never lost, My dear.
It's just now that you seek Me, you've begun to see clear.
You think you're knocking on my door?
No, I've really been knocking on yours,
But I cannot enter by force, of course.
And you can never change what you don't acknowledge.

It's like never changing the oil in a car but running up the mileage
Or having glasses and never agreeing you need them to see
Or having a Savior and never accepting Me.
The clouds, the stars, the wind, and the trees are all signs in unity that I am real.
I'm Here.

But the greatest sign of all is you, My dear.
So, never give up on yourself because I never will.
Please see that now, I need you to never give up on Me.
I'm Here.

Jeremiah 29:13
"And ye shall seek me, and find me, when ye shall search for me with all your heart."

Written By: **Enola Marie Lemon**
(Mother)

Enola Marie Lemon